65p

IN
HISTORY
AIRCRAFT

Authors:

David Smith and Derek Newton

Illustrated by E. A. Hodges

SCHOFIELD & SIMS LTD., HUDDERSFIELD

©1971 Schofield & Sims Ltd.

0 7217 1535 4

0 7217 1565 6   Net edition

Printed in England by Stott Bros. Ltd., Halifax.

First impression 1971
Second impression 1972
Third impression 1974

Clément Ader

The first heavier-than-air machine to lift itself off the ground was built in 1890 by a Frenchman, Clément Ader. His aeroplane was driven by a steam engine and was called the *Eole*. It stayed in the air for about 50 metres.

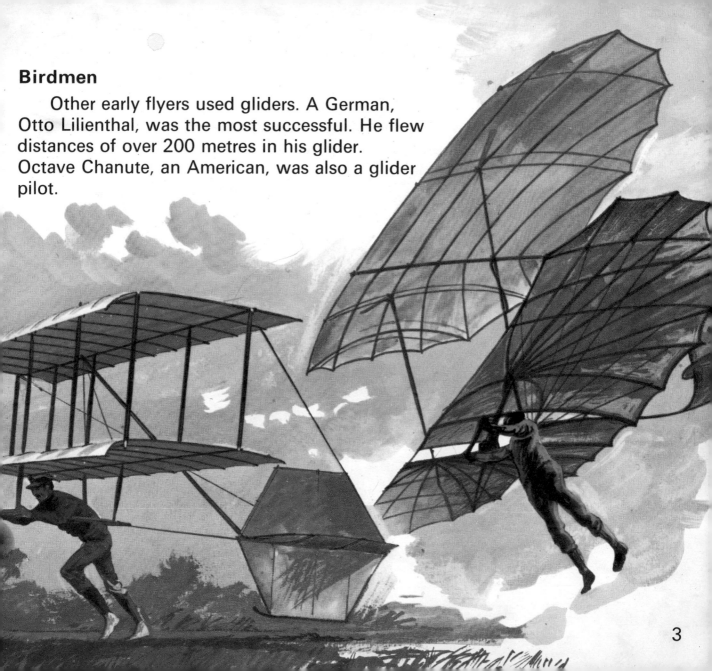

Birdmen

Other early flyers used gliders. A German, Otto Lilienthal, was the most successful. He flew distances of over 200 metres in his glider. Octave Chanute, an American, was also a glider pilot.

3

Wright Brothers

In 1903 two Americans Wilbur and Orville
Wright built their aeroplane the *Flyer*. The *Flyer* had
one of the newly invented petrol engines to drive
its propellers. On December 17th the Wright
Brothers became the first men to make a controlled
powered flight.

Santos-Dumont

The first man to fly an aeroplane in Europe was a Brazilian, Alberto Santos-Dumont. His aeroplane the *14 Bis* flew tail first. Dumont's best flight was over 250 metres in 1906.

S. F. Cody

S. F. Cody, an American, was the first person to fly an aeroplane in Britain. His aeroplane was called the *Cathedral*. In October 1908 he flew this plane for more than 400 metres at Laffon's Plain, near Farnborough. The following year Cody became a British subject.

6

Louis Blériot

Louis Blériot, a Frenchman, became the first man to fly across the English Channel, in 1909. Most aeroplanes at this time had two sets of wings and were called *biplanes*; but Blériot's aeroplane was a *monoplane*.

7

First British Aeroplane

J. T. C. Moore-Brabazon was the first Englishman to fly in Britain. However, his aeroplane was French, so A. V. Roe was the first Briton to fly using his own machine. A. V. Roe also built the first aeroplane with an enclosed cabin.

The Seaplane

The first successful seaplane was built by an American, Glenn Curtiss, in January 1911. Curtiss also built many of the early flying boats. It was a Curtiss flying boat, the N.C.4, which was the first aeroplane to cross the Atlantic.

9

Fighters

During the First World War, 1914–1918,
aircraft improved rapidly. In an air battle, only those
aircraft which were fast and could turn and dive
quickly could survive. The British *Camel,* the
French *Spad* and the German *Fokker* were the
best known fighter planes.

Bombers

Heavy bombers had two or four engines so that they could carry a bigger load of bombs. The Handley Page V/1500 and the Vickers Vimy were British heavy bombers. In 1919 Alcock and Brown made the first non-stop flight across the Atlantic in a Vimy.

The Autogiro

The autogiro was invented in 1923 by Juan de la Cierva, a Spaniard. The propeller drove the aircraft forward. This forward movement caused the four rotor blades to spin round and lift the autogiro off the ground.

First Helicopters

Unlike the autogiro the rotors of a helicopter are driven by the engine. The first successful helicopters were invented by Dr. H. Focke, a German, and Igor Sikorsky, a Russian. These machines took off vertically and could fly forwards, backwards and sideways.

13

First Passenger Planes

The first passenger planes were old bombers. De Havilland 4's flew from London to Paris. Two passengers sat in an open cockpit behind the pilot. They were lent goggles, helmets, gloves, leather coats and even a hot water bottle.

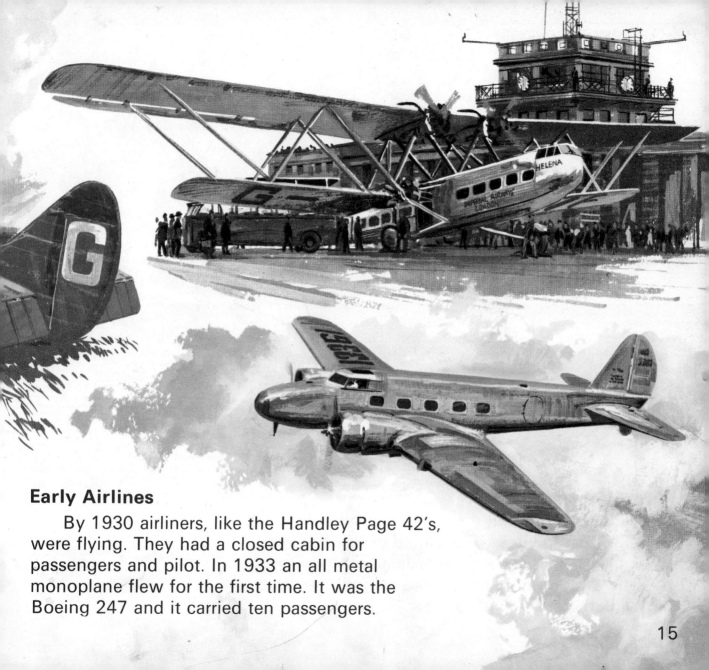

Early Airlines

By 1930 airliners, like the Handley Page 42's, were flying. They had a closed cabin for passengers and pilot. In 1933 an all metal monoplane flew for the first time. It was the Boeing 247 and it carried ten passengers.

Flying Boats

Most places in the world had no airfields so
many passengers were carried in flying boats,
which could land on rivers, lakes, and the sea.
The Short Empire flying boat carried passengers to
all parts of the world.

De Havilland Moth

As flying became safer many flying clubs were formed. The most successful small aeroplane was the De Havilland Moth. It was in a Gipsy Moth that Amy Johnson became the first woman to fly solo to Australia in 1930.

Fighters

During the Second World War, bomber and fighter aircraft were very important. In the Battle of Britain in 1940 the Hurricanes and Spitfires became known for the wonderful way they fought the German Messerschmitts, Dorniers, Junkers and Heinkels.

Bombers

Later in the war the British Lancaster, Halifax and Stirling, and the American Superfortress became just as well known. One unusual aircraft was the Mosquito. Unlike most bombers the Mosquito was made largely of wood.

Heavy Gliders

During the Second World War heavy gliders, like the Horsa, carried airborne troops, light tanks and guns. They were towed until they were over the enemy lines, where they were released to glide to the ground.

First Jet-Aircraft

The first aeroplane to fly using a jet-engine was the German Heinkel He 178 in August 1939. But the first jet-propelled aircraft to go into action in the Second World War was the Gloster Meteor. This British twin-jet fighter joined the battle against Germany's flying bombs in July 1944.

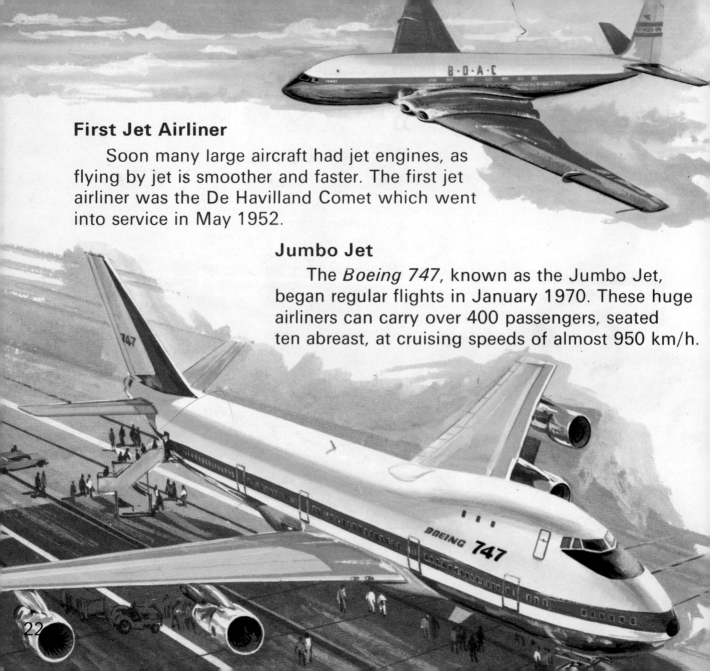

First Jet Airliner

Soon many large aircraft had jet engines, as flying by jet is smoother and faster. The first jet airliner was the De Havilland Comet which went into service in May 1952.

Jumbo Jet

The *Boeing 747*, known as the Jumbo Jet, began regular flights in January 1970. These huge airliners can carry over 400 passengers, seated ten abreast, at cruising speeds of almost 950 km/h.

Aircraft Carriers

Today even aircraft carriers have jet-aircraft.
A Curtis aeroplane was the first to take off and
land on a ship in 1911. The plane took off from a
wooden platform on the deck of an ordinary ship,
but now every navy has specially built aircraft
carriers.

Swept Back Wings

Scientists discovered that aeroplanes which had wings which sloped backwards flew faster than those with ordinary wings. *Swept back* wings were first used in flying wing aircraft like the Vulcan Bomber.

24

Swing Wings

Swept back winged aircraft are more difficult to land than ordinary aircraft. Today there are swing wing planes. On take-off the wings are only slightly swept back, but in the air the wings swing back for high-speed flying.

Argosy

Unusual Aircraft

Today almost anything can be carried by aeroplane. Special freight planes have been built so that loading and unloading can be done very quickly. The noses of the Bristol freighter and the Argosy can be opened and cars can drive straight into the aircraft.

The Canadair 44 has a swing tail.

The Nord 250 has a raised tail so that the back can be opened.

Canadair 44

Nord

27

Modern Helicopters

The modern helicopter has many uses. As it can take off and land without a runway, it can carry people right into busy cities. The army uses helicopters to take wounded soldiers to hospital from the battlefield.

Because helicopters can hover over the same spot
they are useful for rescuing people from the sea.
Police also use them to control traffic.
Some helicopters are so big that they can lift a
heavy lorry, and others can carry forty-three men.

Vertical Take Off XC 142A

The American XC 142A has wings which tilt upwards. With the wings tilted the propellers are like the rotors of a helicopter and they lift the plane vertically. Then the wings return to their normal position for straight flying.

Hawker Siddeley P.1127

The *Hawker Siddeley P.1127* used another way to take off vertically. Whilst the plane was on the ground the jet engines in its wings pointed downwards and thrust the aircraft into the air. Then, as the force of the jets was turned backwards the plane flew forward on its way.

Supersonic Airliner

British and French designers have worked together to build the Concorde jet airliner which will be the fastest airliner in the world. She will carry up to one hundred and thirty-two passengers and will fly from London to New York in less than three and a half hours at a maximum speed of 2250 kilometres per hour.